Rug Chapel
Llangar Church
Gwydir Uchaf Chapel
Derwen Churchyard Cross

W. Nigel Yates MA, PhD, FRHistS

The Historical Background

Introduction

Understandably, the traveller who comes in search of historic monuments in north Wales may be drawn at first to the many great castles situated throughout the ancient kingdom of Gwynedd. There is, however, much of interest besides. Although less famous than their celebrated neighbours, the three picturesque churches looked at in this guidebook were formerly used for Anglican worship, and are now maintained by Cadw. Their particular importance to the nation, to say nothing of their immense charm, rests in the excellent quality of their seventeenth- and eighteenth-century internal furnishings and decoration. Indeed, the survival of such superb liturgical fittings is yet more gratifying when we consider the wholesale transformations which swept through the Anglican church in the second half of the nineteenth century.

It was the 1840s that saw the beginning of the campaign to rebuild, or at least extensively refurbish, the parish churches of England and Wales in a manner that was thought to reproduce their original medieval character. Such were the strength of the campaign and the vigour of its exponents that many of the furnishings installed in these buildings during the seventeenth and eighteenth centuries — and even some genuine medieval fittings — were callously swept away. As a result, only a few examples now survive of Anglican churches which retain internal arrangements that were commonplace before 1840. How fortunate, then, for the north of Wales that it possesses — along with Rug, Llangar and Gwydir Uchaf — one of the largest groups of such churches anywhere in the British Isles.

The three buildings covered by this guide are somewhat different in character. Llangar is an excellent example of a fairly remote and rustic parish church interior, remodelled in the early eighteenth century. Rug and Gwydir Uchaf, however, are the private chapels of wealthy seventeenth-century landowners. They represent the two extremes of Anglican architecture at this time: Rug and Gwydir Uchaf are decidedly 'high church' in their liturgical arrangements, whereas Llangar is more like a Nonconformist chapel of the same period, with the emphasis on the pulpit indicating the importance of preaching rather than the sacrament of Holy Communion. Yet there are also important common features between the three buildings, particularly the western galleries and the paintings which adorned their roofs and walls.

The Reformation in Wales

Church buildings have always been designed in a way that will facilitate the celebration of the services in the manner favoured by those who built them. Before the Reformation the services of churches in England and Wales were much more like those held today in the Orthodox churches of Eastern Europe. The main service, the Mass, was celebrated in Latin — a language most of the laity could not understand —

St Augustine's, Penarth, Vale of Glamorgan, is typical of the familiar nineteenth-century Gothic-style church interior. Such arrangements rapidly replaced the liturgical practices of the seventeenth and eighteenth centuries; survivals such as Rug, Llangar and Gwydir Uchaf are of great significance.

Opposite: The sixteenth-century Reformation of the church led to services in English and, later, Welsh. A simple communion table replaced the altar and preaching became important, as shown in this detail from John Foxe's Book of Martyrs, *1583 (University of Aberdeen).*

Left: In the earlier arrangements, the priest celebrated the Latin service of Mass at the altar, separated from the congregation in the nave, as depicted in this fifteenth-century manuscript detail (Musée de Condé, Chantilly/ Bridgeman Art Library, Ms. 65/1284, f. 158r).

The charming interior of the church of St Issui, Partrishow, Powys. Here, the pre-Reformation arrangement with a wooden screen, which separated the clergy from the laity, still survives. The Partrishow screen is well known for its excellent quality.

The Reformation placed great emphasis on Holy Communion, and the Book of Common Prayer envisaged a weekly celebration in most churches. In practice, many rural parishes in Wales celebrated quarterly. This title page is taken from the 1567 edition of the Book of Common Prayer in Welsh (The National Library of Wales).

and took place in the chancel on the eastern side of the rood screen, with the clergy assisted by those in minor orders. The laity, who occupied the nave, participated in their own devotions assisted by the presence of statues, stained glass in the windows and paintings on the walls. At various important points of the service bells were rung to inform the congregation of what was taking place in the chancel, such as the elevation of the host at the time of consecration.

Changes brought about by the Reformation meant that by the 1540s the old Latin services were replaced by new services, initially in English but eventually also in Welsh. The rood screens and the stone altars in the chancel, as well as other altars in front of the screen or in chantry chapels, were ordered to be demolished and replaced with a simple wooden communion table placed either in the middle of the chancel or at the east end of the nave. In practice, however, in some of the remoter parts of England and Wales, these orders were ignored and some screens, and even a few lofts and stone altars, survived. The preaching of sermons had grown in popularity in the years preceding the Reformation, but the pulpit and the desk from which much of the

service was read became essential pieces of furniture for the new Protestant services. The clergy were no longer separated from the laity and both were expected to participate together in the new services with the former preaching to the latter on a regular basis.

The Reformation in England and Wales seems to have enjoyed the tacit support of most of the population. Nevertheless, a few people retained a preference for the old Latin services and remained Roman Catholics, despite sporadic persecution. Others thought the Reformation, which had preserved much of the administrative structure and some of the liturgical practices of the pre-Reformation church, needed to be taken further. These people were known as Puritans and they put pressure on the government to abolish bishops. They also sought to abolish certain practices in the services of the church, such as the clergy wearing surplices, the use of the sign of the cross at baptism and that of the ring in marriage, which they thought smacked of 'popery'. Both the crown and the bishops were determined to resist these demands and by the 1620s a group of high church bishops gained control of the church and decided to move it back in a somewhat more Catholic direction. The altars were moved back to the east end of the chancels and fenced in with altar rails. Two candles were frequently placed on the altar, though not usually lit, and a reredos was formed from panels containing suitable scriptural texts and pictures behind the altar; even screens were reintroduced. Although these changes suffered a setback during the Civil War (1642–48) and Commonwealth, they were reintroduced after 1660 and generally remained in force until the early nineteenth century.

Worship in the Seventeenth and Eighteenth Centuries

The Book of Common Prayer had envisaged that the Holy Communion would be celebrated at least weekly in most churches. However, the unwillingness of the laity to attend communion services regularly, together with the need for a minimum requirement of three communicants, meant that there was a celebration only quarterly in many (especially rural) parishes. In others, particularly urban ones, communion was perhaps celebrated monthly.

On the majority of Sundays, however, the usual morning service consisted of Morning Prayer, Litany, Ante-Communion and Sermon, a service which lasted on average for a little less than two hours. Evening Prayer would have been held in the afternoon, probably with catechizing rather than a full sermon, but not all churches had two Sunday services. All services apart from Holy Communion would have been conducted from the reading desk, usually placed either opposite or adjacent to the pulpit, with the responses led by the parish clerk. Before the eighteenth century the music in churches tended to consist solely of metrical versions of the psalms or canticles. The parish clerk would sing each line and the congregation would then repeat the line. This would have been done without musical accompaniment. This practice survived in the Church of Scotland until well into the nineteenth century but it is now confined to a few Presbyterian churches in the western highlands and islands.

By the eighteenth century most parishes had a band of singers and musicians, or in town churches an organ, which normally occupied a gallery at the west

The 1630s saw a greater emphasis on ritual in the services of the church with the consequent reintroduction of features such as altar rails, candles and a reredos. Despite a temporary setback during the Civil War (1642–48), as depicted in this contemporary engraving, these changes were re-established after 1660 (Ashmolean Museum).

Below: Singers, such as those shown in this nineteenth-century cartoon, would sometimes have occupied a gallery situated at the west end of many churches (British Library).

After the Nicene Creed the minister, who would have worn a full-length surplice for the rest of the service, would have changed into a black gown and ascended into the pulpit to preach, or, in many cases, to read somebody else's sermon. Welsh congregations were particularly appreciative of a good sermon, and were inclined to complain if the sermon was omitted, as it occasionally was when one clergyman served more than one church.

When the Holy Communion was celebrated, the normal custom was for the celebrant to proceed to the altar at the offertory and to be followed by the rest of the communicants, who would position themselves as near as possible to the altar. In churches where there was not room for the communicants to 'draw near', they might be communicated at the altar rails at the appropriate time, or the minister might bring the communion around to the people in their seats. In some churches the altar stood in the middle of the chancel and there were seats for communicants all around the walls on three sides.

As a result of the various reform movements in the church in the nineteenth century, many of these liturgical practices — which had existed for the best part of three centuries — were swept away. The most important change was the breaking up of the morning service into separate services of Morning Prayer and Holy Communion. Sermons became shorter and were usually preached in a surplice instead of the black gown. Music became even more important in the worship of the church and the choir was usually placed, vested in surplices, in the chancel. Reading desks were replaced by much smaller clergy stalls, pulpits were reduced in size, box pews replaced by open benches, and the whole visual emphasis placed on the altar at the east end of the chancel.

Because of the speed with which these changes were accomplished, those churches that have survived more or less intact from the seventeenth and eighteenth centuries may look odd to those for whom the concept of the church interior immediately conjures up the Gothicism of nineteenth-century architects like Sir George Gilbert Scott (d. 1878) or George Edmund Street (d. 1881). Yet it is these strange preaching houses that represent an earlier liturgical tradition created by the Reformation of the sixteenth century.

end of the church. During the course of the eighteenth century parish choirs attempted to sing more elaborate settings of the psalms and canticles, with usually an anthem on festivals or sacrament Sundays. From the early nineteenth century rural churches began to disband their groups of musicians and replace them with organs, frequently of the barrel variety, though these had their limitations as the number of tunes they could play was somewhat restricted.

In the seventeenth century it was customary for the minister to conduct the Ante-Communion from the north side of the altar, but by the eighteenth century this practice had been abandoned and the whole morning service, including the reading of the lessons, was conducted from the reading desk.

Church Building after the Reformation

In order that we can place Rug, Llangar and Gwydir Uchaf in context, it is as well for us to look at the liturgical arrangement of Anglican churches before 1840. In broad terms, such arrangements fell into one of six main types, depending on the relationship between altar, pulpit, reading desk and seating. The first type represented a minimal change in the arrangements of the medieval church. The chancel or altar space was still separated from the nave, and the pulpit and reading desk placed in either the north-east or south-east corner of the nave. This arrangement survives at a number of north Wales churches, including Carnguwch, Llandygwnning, Llanfrothen, Penllech and Worthenbury.

In the second type of church an attempt was made to create a single liturgical focus at the east end, with the pulpit and reading desk placed either behind or in front of the altar. No Anglican instances of this type of arrangement survive in Wales, though there are a few in England and Ireland. A complete Nonconformist example does, none the less, survive in the Caebach chapel of 1715 at Llandrindod Wells.

The third type of church, of which Llangar is a good example, is one in which the pulpit and reading desk are placed about halfway down one of the long walls of the nave, so that the seats can be arranged to face them, even if this means they face away from the altar, and the minister can be seen and heard in all parts of the church. Another fine example of this type of church in north Wales is Llanddoged, rebuilt as late as 1838–39. The interior is dominated by a massive pulpit and reading desk, flanked on one side by the royal arms of Queen Victoria, and on the other by a picture of the prophet Isaiah, with the legend 'preach the Gospel' in Welsh. There are other examples of such churches at Llanfigael and Llangwyllog, and a Nonconformist example at Capel Newydd, Nanhoron.

Below left: Worthenbury church, Wrexham. Here, the arrangement of the church differs little from its medieval predecessors. The nave and chancel remain separate but the reading desk and pulpit are located in the south-east corner of the nave.

Bottom left: Caebach chapel, Llandrindod Wells, Powys. It is a Nonconformist example of an attempt to create a single liturgical focus (Photograph by Paul Hughes).

Below right: Llanddoged church, Conwy. As at Llangar, the pulpit and reading desk are positioned so the minister can be seen and heard in all parts of the church.

Llanfaglan church, Gwynedd, which shows the radical arrangement of a T-shape plan. There are seats in both the nave and transept, all of which face the large tiered pulpit and reading desk (David Toase).

The fourth and most radical type of liturgical arrangement was the T-plan church, with long transepts and seating in both nave and transepts facing the pulpit and reading desk. Churches of this type were very common in the north-west corner of Wales. Those that retain largely unaltered contemporary fittings include Dolwyddelan (1711), Llanfaglan (1769), Ynyscynhaearn (1830–32), Capel Curig (1839) and Betws-y-Coed (1843). It is noticeable how late such churches continued to be built in the remoter parts of Wales and this has undoubtedly contributed to their better survival here than in some other parts of the British Isles.

The fifth type of church was one where, as at Gwydir Uchaf, the seating was placed along the sides of the church as in a college chapel. Another good example of such a church in north Wales is Llandwrog, rebuilt by Lord Newborough in 1860.

In the sixth type of church, pulpit and reading desk are physically separated and are designed to stand one on either side of the altar space, or the entrance to the chancel. There are several surviving examples in north Wales, at Betws-yn-Rhos (1838–39), Aberdaron and Llanffinan (both 1841), Llanarmon Dyffryn Ceiriog (1846), and the particularly late examples at Llangwyfan (1859) and Llandyfrydog (1862).

Rug and Gwydir Uchaf chapels belong to a group of four private chapels erected in north Wales in the seventeenth century, all of which have escaped complete alteration. The other two examples are the Jesus chapel at Llanfair Dyffryn Clwyd and the Gwydir chapel at Llanrwst. Of the four, the earliest is the Jesus chapel, founded in 1619 and consecrated in 1623 to serve as a combined chapel for Morning and Evening Prayer on Sundays and for use as a schoolroom during the week. It is, however, the most substantially altered of the four buildings, having been largely rebuilt in 1787 and partly refurbished in 1941. The Gwydir chapel is attached to Llanrwst parish church and was built in 1633–34. It served as a family pew and burial aisle and may also have been used for weekday services by the inmates of the Jesus Hospital founded in 1612 by Sir John Wynn of Gwydir. The dedication of chapels to Jesus and the Holy Trinity, rather than to individual saints, was a feature of Anglican practice in the seventeenth century, though a return to the earlier practice of dedicating churches to popular saints, such as George, John the Evangelist or the Virgin Mary, had returned by the eighteenth century.

Location of Churches and Chapels Mentioned in the Text

Llanfigael
Llandyfrydog
Llangwyllog
Llanffinan
Gyffin
Trelawnyd
Betws-yn-Rhos
Llanddoged
Llangwyfan
Gwydir Uchaf Chapel
Gwydir Chapel, Llanrwst
Llanfaglan
Llanrhydd
Capel Curig
Llanynys
Llandwrog
Betws-y-Coed
Dolwyddelan
Jesus Chapel, Llanfair Dyffryn Clwyd
Derwen
Carnguwch
Llanfrothen
Rug Chapel
Worthenbury
Penllech
Ynyscynhaearn
Llangar Church
Corwen
Llandygwnning
Capel Newydd, Nanhoron
Hanmer
Aberdaron
Llanarmon Dyffryn Ceiriog

N

Private chapels ●
Churches/chapels ■

| 0 | 15 | 30 Kilometres |
| 0 | 10 | 20 Miles |

Caebach Chapel, Llandrindod Wells

Far left: Llandwrog church, Gwynedd. As at Gwydir Uchaf, the seating is arranged along the sides of the church (David Toase).

Left: Llanarmon Dyffryn Ceiriog church, Wrexham. Here, the pulpit and reading desk are physically separate and stand on either side of the altar.

The Gwydir chapel, attached to Llanrwst parish church, was built in 1633–34 as the private chapel for the Wynn family, who later built Gwydir Uchaf chapel (Janet and Colin Bord/Fortean Picture Library).

A History of Rug Chapel

The private chapel of Holy Trinity at Rug, in the parish of Corwen, was built in 1637 by Colonel William Salusbury (1580–1660), a colourful character who led a full and active life. During the Civil War, as a staunch royalist and governor of Denbigh Castle, the colonel was most famous for his defence of the stronghold against the parliamentarians from 1643 to 1646.

From the twelfth to the sixteenth centuries, the lordship of Rug belonged to the descendants of Madog ap Maredudd (d. 1160), prince of Powys. Eventually, the Welsh heiress married Piers Salusbury of Bachymbyd, the owner of important estates in Denbighshire. In 1549 their son, Robert Salusbury, purchased the lordship of Glyndyfrdwy, which had once belonged to Owain Glyn Dŵr, and the estates were further enlarged in 1635 with the marriage of Owen Salusbury (d. 1657/1658) — son of the chapel builder — to the wealthy heiress, Mary Goodman of Abenbury. The failure of Owen Salusbury to produce a male heir led to his estates eventually passing to the Vaughans of Nannau and, later, to the ubiquitous Wynn family.

Very little is known of the history of Rug chapel. The deed of endowment, dated 3 January 1641, laid down:

that one discreet and competently learned scholar of good carriage and behaviour, being a distinct and sensible reader, and being a minister and within Holy Orders, to be from time to time chosen, nominated and appointed by the said William Salusbury and his heirs, be admitted and employed from time to time for ever to be curate of or reader in the said Chapel, and to officiate therein, and to read and celebrate Divine Service and other Holy exercises therein in the native and vulgarly known tongue there, both morning and evening, upon all Sundays, Holidays and Festival days, and at all other times whensoever Divine Service is or ought to be read or celebrated…according to the ceremonies of the Church of England.

The curate was not to serve or undertake any other cure, and could be removed by the patrons for neglect of duty. If the patrons failed to appoint a successor within six months the patronage was to lapse for that turn to the bishop of St Asaph, but even his appointee could be removed by the patrons for neglect of duty. The endowment was provided by two messuages in Mustwyr, then or late in the tenure of Thomas Wynne, gentleman, and Ellis ap Roger respectively, lying between the rivers Terfynnant and Afon Eglwyseg, the Berwyn mountains and the river Dee, together with the meadows in Rug called Hirdir Gwiail. These lands were to provide an annual income of £12, to be administered by trustees empowered to fill vacancies in their number as they occurred.

During the eighteenth and nineteenth centuries, the original terms of the endowment were overlooked and the chaplaincy of Rug was normally held by the vicars of Corwen or rectors of the neighbouring

Opposite: Rug chapel, built in 1637 as the private chapel for Colonel William Salusbury (1580–1660), stands in a pastoral setting just outside Corwen.

The deed of endowment for Rug chapel, dated 3 January 1641 and signed by William and Owen Salusbury, in which provision is made for the appointment of a curate to celebrate Divine Service 'in the native and vulgarly known tongue' (The National Library of Wales).

parish of Llangar. Samuel Lewis, in his *A Topographical Dictionary of Wales* (1838), noted also that 'the English service only is performed' at Rug, not the service in Welsh as originally intended. In 1859, the then patron, Sir Robert Vaughan of Rug, left a sum of £200 to the bishop of St Asaph, the income from which was to be used to augment the stipend paid to the chaplain.

In 1861–62 the chaplaincy was worth £90 per annum and the chaplain was expected to conduct two services each Sunday. The jurisdictional status of Rug chapel seems to have been that of a peculiar. The chapel appears never to have been consecrated and was considered exempt from visitation both by the bishop and the rural dean, though it clearly fulfilled a quasi-parochial function. In 1730 it was noted that 'great numbers of people resort thither besides the family of Rug'. The chapel was not licensed for marriages and a special dispensation had to be obtained by a member of the Wynn family to be

married there in 1873. Thomas Vowler Short, bishop of St Asaph 1846–70, commented: 'you Rug chaplains are my curates and you are not my curates. I have no control over you but as long as you are licensed to me, there's a sort of responsibility'.

Sir Stephen Glynne visited Rug chapel on 21 November 1849, and recorded the following remarks in his notebook: 'An interesting building, as a specimen of a chapel built in 1637. It consists of one space, without distinction of chancel; a small belfry over the west end; the windows ugly, having mullions, and no tracery; and the entrance at the west end. The roof is a very fair, open timber one, of decidedly Gothic work, and very much resembling those described at Gwyddelwern and Derwen. The brackets stand on shafts, and are enriched with angels with displayed wings. The whole roof is covered with colour, and has gilt stars on a blue ground. The cornice has rather a debased character. The whole of the walls, as well as

Rug chapel, as drawn by John Ingleby in 1794. The picture shows the debased Gothic windows which were later remodelled by Sir Robert Vaughan in 1854–55 (The National Library of Wales).

A watercolour sketch of the interior of Rug chapel, prior to the construction of the chancel screen by Sir Robert Vaughan during the 1854–55 restoration work (By courtesy of Lord Newborough).

the roof, is covered with various colours, with some grotesque paintings and scrolls bearing texts in Welsh. The altar is formed by a chest, and the rails which enclose it open at the sides, contrary to usual custom. On the north and south of the east end are covered seats, also painted, used as pulpit and reading-pew. There are also some plain open benches, but no font'.

In 1854–55 Sir Robert Vaughan restored the exterior of the building, remodelling the windows and the bell turret. The east window, by N. H. J. Westlake (1833–1921), dates from 1896 and was commissioned by C. H. Wynn (d. 1911).

Rug also inspired the work of the famous architect, Edwin Lutyens (1869–1944), who visited the chapel as a young man with Herbert Baker (1862–1946) in 1888. He later wrote to Baker of his recollections of Rug, 'painted by some Jacobean — red and blue' and 'a delicious old chandelier, all made of wood painted green', remembered when designing similar fittings for the Viceroy's House at Delhi. The bench ends at Rug apparently also inspired Lutyens to use curious indented beams to link the pews at Campion Hall, Oxford.

The east window, designed by the celebrated Victorian painter, designer and writer on art, N. H. J Westlake (1833–1921).

A Tour of Rug Chapel

Architecturally, as we shall see, Rug chapel is an excellent example of early seventeenth-century church design and furnishing. As such, it very much represents an extension of late medieval church design. The roof in particular may be compared with late fifteenth- and early sixteenth-century carved and painted roofs, of which it is a logical continuation, though with more classical features — common in furniture of the 1600s — revealed in the intricate panels of the cornice (inside front cover).

Visitors who go on to Gwydir Uchaf chapel will see the real revolution in church decoration. There (pp. 41–45) the furnishings are fully classical in style, and the painted ceiling is unashamedly baroque.

The Grounds and Exterior

Since work began on the conservation of the chapel, a good deal of attention has been paid to its landscape setting. From the reception building, the visitor's path leads to a semi-formal entrance marked by stone gateposts, which have been moved to their present position from alongside the main road. Once through the gateway, the scene is one to delight the senses, both by the fragrances and colours. The path continues, bordered by lavenders, towards a stone cross.

Standing on three dry-built steps, the cross shaft rises almost 6 feet (1.8m) high. The cross itself is almost certainly that which appears on the east gable of the chapel in Ingleby's drawing of 1794 (p. 12), since the rebate for the ridge slates can still be seen on one face. The cross is traditionally said to have been brought from Denbigh Castle by Colonel Salusbury.

Facing the chapel, with a bed of shrubs to the left, and the cross to the right, the vista ahead is charming. The low beds of heathers and herbs take the eye to the west front of the building, whereas high in the distance are the earthworks which mark the prehistoric hillfort enclosure of Caer Drewyn.

When considering the exterior of the chapel itself, we should be aware that it was reconstructed in 1854–55. A small vestry was added at the north-east corner and all the windows renewed. The original chapel consisted of the small nave and chancel under one roof, there being no external or interior structural division between the two. The drawing of the exterior in 1794, by J. Ingleby, shows that it then had very debased Gothic windows which may have been the original ones (as mentioned by Glynne in 1849, p. 12). The Victorian reconstruction was correct but uninspired, very much in line with the somewhat mediocre restorations generally prevalent in Wales at that time. The entrance is in the centre of the west wall under a bellcote.

The Interior of the Chapel

Fittings

The rather plain and austere external appearance of Rug gives no clue to the sheer delights of the interior. The fittings and decoration were little altered in the 1854–55 reconstruction, or subsequently, and the chapel retains most of its original 1637 features. It is, therefore, a rare example of an interior dating from the

The stone cross in the grounds of Rug. It is traditionally said to have been brought from Denbigh Castle by Colonel Salusbury.

Opposite: The path through the low beds of heathers and herbs leads to the principal entrance in the west front of Rug chapel.

One of the four wooden angels which decorate the base of two of the roof trusses at Rug. The angel is carved in relief and is supported on a projecting bracket.

Rug Chapel: Ground Plan

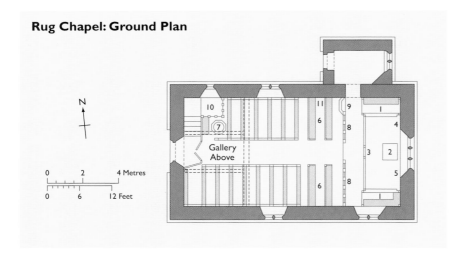

'high church' liturgical experiments of King Charles I's reign (1625–49), which are reflected in its design.

The principal contemporary fittings in the chancel are the handsome canopied pews (**1**) on each side of the altar (**2**). There has been some debate about the origin of these, and it has been maintained that one was always intended to be used as a reading pew by the chaplain and that the other formed a 'houseling' pew, used by intending communicants during the final part of the Prayer Book service. Neither suggestion seems likely; the pews are too large for the former function and too small for the latter. It would seem much more likely that they were the pews used by the patrons and their families. Canopied family pews were fairly common in the seventeenth century and there are two remarkably similar to those at Rug, and in exactly the same position, at Easton Church in Suffolk. What, however, does seem likely is that, in the absence of a reading desk or pulpit, the service was always conducted by the chaplain from the western end of one of those pews. When Stapleford Church in Leicestershire was built in 1783 it also had neither pulpit nor reading desk, and the chaplain conducted the service from the west gallery that also served as the family pew.

The altar rails (**3**) are also seventeenth century, placed in their present position within recent years. There are traces of mortice holes on the east side of the end posts, and it appears that at one time the rails surrounded the altar on three sides. There are indications, too, that the rails were initially longer. This perhaps suggests that they may not be original to Rug, as they do not appear to fit.

The design of the sanctuary chair (**4**) is seventeenth century, as is the date of the interesting triangular credence table (**5**), dated 1632. The last piece is almost certainly a section from a former domestic table, but it is not clear whether it was placed in its present position in 1637, when credence tables were approved of in principle by 'high churchmen' though rarely used in practice, or whether it appeared subsequently, as credence tables gradually became an accepted part of a church's furniture. Such small tables are generally situated to the side of the altar, and the bread and wine placed on them at the beginning of the communion service.

The altar and tiled sanctuary were installed in the late nineteenth or early twentieth centuries, as were the stained-glass windows throughout the church.

Above right: One of the two canopied pews, which flank the altar in the chancel.

Right: The seventeenth-century credence table within the altar rails at Rug chapel. It is dated 1632.

There is seventeenth-century wooden panelling on the lower parts of the nave walls, which are plastered above. At the east end of the nave, on each side, are two tall typical seventeenth-century pews (**6**). Behind them are two sets (six on the north, and eight on the south) of open benches of an extremely unusual design. The benches, which were originally plain seats, were widened and given their crude backs in the late nineteenth century. They are joined together at their bases and the remarkable carvings of animals and birds on these joining sections are of seventeenth-century workmanship (see inside front cover). A similar, though less elaborate, series of benches has survived at Dolwyddelan church.

The nave floor was retiled in the nineteenth century and the plain font (**7**) dates from 1864. At the restoration of 1854–55 the nave and chancel were effectively separated by a new chancel screen (**8**). This in itself is an interesting piece of work, having been deliberately designed in a mock-Jacobean style to harmonize with the genuine seventeenth-century fittings, which it does very successfully. The northern section of this screen was also provided with an ingenious lectern-pulpit (**9**), the front of which is inscribed with three appropriate (but subtly adapted) biblical texts, reading from left to right: two verses from the Epistles (1 Thessalonians 5: 17 and part of James 5: 16) and Psalm 51: 17; a 'Christianized' version of Psalm 19: 14; and an adaptation of Matthew 11: 28. At the west end of the nave the seventeenth-century gallery, reached by a panelled staircase (**10**) in the north-west corner of the building, has a nicely carved balustrade and benches contemporary with those seen below. Until recently, much of the south-west corner of the gallery was occupied by an organ and its piping, now removed and leaving a blank area of walling.

The Roof

The original unity of the chapel is maintained by the survival of its finest feature, the magnificent carved and coloured roof. The bulk of the decoration is undoubtedly original, though in examining the detail we should bear in mind a description by Thomas Price, one of the mid-nineteenth-century chaplains at Rug. From his observations, it seems some repainting may have taken place around 1750–80.

The roof itself is supported on five principal trusses. The sides of these trusses are delightfully painted with a flowing floral design, with further

Above: The ornate interior of Rug chapel, looking east from the gallery towards the altar.

Left: The lectern-pulpit at Rug was incorporated into the chancel screen, erected during the restoration of 1854–55. The texts are adapted from two verses from the Epistles (1 Thessalonians 5: 17 and part of James 5: 16) and Psalm 51: 17; Psalm 19: 14; and Matthew 11: 28.

decoration on the panels of the roof itself. The fine carved and coloured roof bosses include a variety of emblems such as thistles, flowers, a goat, and the sacred Christian emblem, IHS. This is the abbreviated form of the name of Jesus in Greek, sometimes taken in the western church to be an acronym for *Iesus, Hominum Salvator* (Jesus, Saviour of Humankind). The east truss, above the altar, is inscribed with the date 1637, which was later overpainted. Above the chancel screen, the feet of the next truss are decorated with painted crowned angels.

Yet more elaborate is the series of four charming cut-out wooden angels supported on brackets which project from the base of two of the trusses. They are similar to those at Gwydir Uchaf, though here at Rug they are carved in relief. In turn, on both sides, the roof trusses are set into an elaborate wooden cornice — or frieze — which runs the full length of the chapel from east to west. The variety of carving, including strange whimsical monsters, is quite intriguing and we can only guess at its meaning to the artist, or to William Salusbury himself.

Suspended from the middle of the central roof truss is an unusual painted wooden candelabrum, which has been restored. The fact that the truss is flattened suggests that it was always intended to hang at this point. At the top are four carved and painted cherubs, and below are two tiers of radial arms for candle holders: six above and twelve at the bottom.

The Wall Decoration

At the east end of the north wall of the nave is a very unusual seventeenth-century wall painting (11). It consists of two tall Corinthian pilasters crudely painted in perspective standing on a podium, the whole reaching the full height of the wall. The main painting is contained in an oblong panel with small fluted Ionic pilasters from which spring small arches containing leaf decoration.

The painting portrays the familiar theme of the transient nature of our sojourn on earth and the inevitability of death. Lavish use has been made of the emblems traditionally associated with the subject. A central white panel or table top has at each end a painted turned candlestick with a lighted candle. Nearer the centre are an hourglass and a dial on which is painted *fugit hora* (the hour flies). The main feature of the upper part is a skull surrounded by a wreath or garland containing seven roses. The lower

part is occupied by a skeleton reclining on a pillow of coiled rope. Between the hourglass and the dial is the Latin inscription *ut hora sic vita* (as with the hour so with life). Beneath this are inscriptions in Welsh:

val i treila r tân gan bwull, gwur y ganwull gynudd. fellu r enioes ar rhod sudd yn darfod beunudd.

This is an excerpt from a carol by Richard Gwyn, a Roman Catholic martyr executed in 1584. It translates 'as the flame gradually consumes the tallow of the lighted candle so life on the orbit (earth) perishes daily.'

yrhoedel er hyd a for aros a derfudd yn udd ag yn nos.

These are the last two lines of one of the *Englynion y Misoedd* and translate as 'lifetime, however long its stay, will come to an end by night and by day'.

Darfu fynrwyn am wuneb mud iawn wy nim edwyn neb.

This is a quotation from a *cywydd* (a form of poem) attributed to Ieuan ap Rhydderch which translates as 'my nose and my face are perished, very dumb am I, no one knows me'.

pob cadarn: gwan i ddiwedd

A proverb first recorded in 1547 and meaning 'every strong one is weak in the end'.

There are several other Welsh inscriptions on the walls of the interior, or on the furnishings, all taken from the Bible published by William Morgan in 1588 (see illustration, p. 22), the revised translation of 1620, or the 1621 edition of the Welsh Prayer Book. They are all painted in Gothic or Roman lettering, with minuscules, but it is impossible to date them precisely.

Above: The title page of the 1621 Welsh edition of the Book of Common Prayer. A number of the inscriptions found in Rug chapel were taken from this text, or from the 1588 and 1620 editions of the Welsh Bible (British Library).

Opposite: Part of the decorated ceiling looking towards the gallery. An unusual painted wooden candelabrum is suspended from the central roof truss.

Below: The inscriptions and graphic depiction of a skull and skeleton in this unusual seventeenth-century wall painting at Rug reflect the familiar theme of the transient nature of life and the inevitability of death.

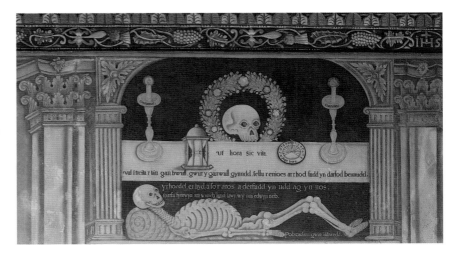

A History of Llangar Church and Parish

Origins to the Seventeenth Century

The origins of the parish church of All Saints at Llangar are obscure, as is the meaning of the place name. According to the Reverend John Wynne, writing in 1730, the original form was Llann-Garw-Gwyn, or 'the church of the white deer'. The reason for this, he tells us, was that a white deer was disturbed in a thicket on the spot where the church stood, and in tradition the boundaries of the parish were determined by the directions in which the deer ran. Samuel Lewis, writing in 1838, put forward the less romantic view that the name was originally Llangaer or 'the church of the camp'. This, he suggested, was 'derived from an ancient fortification which formerly occupied the summit of the hill called Caer Wern, in the immediate vicinity of the church, and of which there are still some vestiges, though nothing is known of its origin or history'.

In fact there is a prehistoric hilltop enclosure called Y Gaerwen at the summit of Y Foel, but this is more than a mile (1.6km) from the church and on the other side of the river. The church was assessed in the *Taxatio Ecclesiastica* of 1291 at the nominal value of £4. By then, however, it was already an independent parish church not connected with any major family, but firmly in the patronage of the bishop of St Asaph, in the western extremities of whose diocese it lay. In the *Valor Ecclesiasticus* of 1535 the rectory of Llangar was valued at the more precise sum of £5 7s. 8d., around the average for Welsh livings at the time. These are in fact the only pre-Reformation references

to the church, since very few of the medieval records of the diocese of St Asaph have survived. There is, however, no historical evidence to suggest that the church at Llangar was a particularly early ecclesiastical foundation, nor was anything to the contrary revealed by the archaeological excavation of 1974 (p. 26). The dedication alone would point to a likely foundation date in the twelfth or early thirteenth centuries.

By 1682, the main part of the parish had been divided into two townships, Cymer and Llangar, with the further detached township of Gwnodl separated from the rest by the intervening parish of Gwyddelwern. The church and churchyard walls were repaired by the parish, but parts of the walls were to be maintained by the families living in the two small gentry houses in the parish, Gwerclas and Plas Isaf. All the tithes of the parish were paid in kind, except that 2d. was owed for every odd lamb over any number divisible by ten, and 3d. was paid in lactuals (a tax levied on unweaned animals) for each calf and foal. By an agreement of 4 September 1538 the parish, along with others in the rural deanery of Penllyn and Edeirnion, had been allowed to keep these lactual dues, originally paid to the bishop, in return for an annual cash payment: 8s. 8d. in the case of Llangar. The parish also paid an annual sum of 6s. to the bishop, and 4s. in 'procurations' every third year during the bishop's visitation of the diocese. At Easter the parish received 5d. from every marriage, 4d. from every tradesman, and 3d. from every widow and hired servant, in statutory dues; the sexton received in addition 2d. from every marriage and widow. The family of Gwerclas rented part of the glebe from the rector at an annual rate of 11s.

Opposite: The huge figure of Death on the north wall of Llangar church, opposite the main entrance, would have greeted parishioners and reminded them of the transience of life.

This entry, taken from the Valor Ecclesiasticus *of 1535, records that Llangar church was valued at £5 7s. 8d. (The National Archives: PRO, E344/19/8).*

Part of the Reverend John Wynne's 1730 survey of Llangar church. The survey provides valuable insights into the condition of the church at the time (The National Library of Wales, SA/RD21).

The title page of the first edition of the Welsh Bible, translated and produced by William Morgan in 1588. In 1753 it was noted that Llangar Church still only possessed Welsh versions of the Bible and Prayer Book (The National Library of Wales).

Eighteenth-Century Descriptions and Surveys

The first full description of the church dates from a survey made in 1730. The church then measured 60 feet by (scarcely) 15 feet (9.1m by 4.6m). It had been newly plastered outside, but inside the plaster was 'miserably decay'd, dirty and foul' and it was hoped to replaster the interior shortly. The paintings on the walls — including the Lord's Prayer, Creed, Royal Arms and Sentences — were almost defaced. The Ten Commandments hung from the roof on boards but the rural dean ordered they should be painted on the east wall. The chancel formed almost half the church and had, within the altar rails, the reading desk situated on the south-east side. Also within the rails, there was a pew erected by the Reverend Mr Eyton, the late rector and vicar of Corwen and owner of Plas Isaf, then tenanted by an attorney, Robert Owens.

The pulpit was on the north wall, outside the chancel and opposite the south door. Beneath it was a pew, the ownership of which was disputed between Robert Owens and the present rector. There were only two other pews in the nave. The north wall had only one window, said to have been recently enlarged, there were three 'little pigeon holes' in the south wall, which Archdeacon Thomas in 1874 thought might be a rare triple piscina, and the east window was 'not of the usual nor indeed of a becoming size'. There was a spacious gallery at the

west end with benches in good repair. The floor of the church slanted heavily downwards from the east to the west end and was roughly flagged. The service was read every Sunday and Holy Day and the sacrament administered monthly. The parish had only one pauper to support and no chapels or known dissenters. The yearly profit of the rectory was reckoned at £70 excluding offerings, described as considerable. By 1732 the church had undergone substantial alteration:

The churchyard was new fenced last year, and has a handsome gate and stile leading to it. The church walls and roof were both lately mended, and are in very good order. The windows are whole and lightsome and ye walls within new wash'd and painted, and ye floor flagg'd. Ye gallery is an ordinary piece of work, but very strong and large and ye benches in it all good. The body of ye church consists mostly of benches, which are all well framed and uniform, and what few seats they have are in good repair and order. The pulpit is large and handsome, it stands in a good light, and is covered with a very good cloth and cushion. Ye font stands just below ye pulpit, and is of a good size and well covered. The communion table is well rail'd and has three benches within ye rails, one whereof is common, another is a property. The third belongs to ye Rector's family. There are benches and seats erected so close to ye Rails of ye Altar, that there is no room for the communicants to come up, but ye minister is obliged to go along ye church to administer the Elements to ye Congregation. The Reading Seat, which is ye handsomest in all ye Deanery stands likewise within ye Rails of ye Alter. The Bible is perfect and well bound, the Common Prayer book something torn in ye morning and evening service, otherwise perfect and clear. The surplice is new and fine. Ye communion table is large and decent and covered with a green cloth. The linnen which are a diaper table cloth and napkin, are fresh and good. The Plate are a small silver chalice and cover: a flaggon, salver and a plate, all of pewter. Ye church chest, bier and bier cloth are all very good in their kind.

In 1753 it was noted that the church only possessed a Welsh Bible and Prayer Book — presumably this had been the case in 1732, but it had not been thought worth noting. By 1775, however, Llangar had acquired an English Bible and Prayer Book, presented by Mrs Lloyd of Gwerclas.

The parish of Llangar appears to have had a remarkably stable and uneventful history during the eighteenth and early nineteenth centuries. In every visitation or parochial return from 1730 until 1834, the service was noted as being read every Sunday and Holy Day, and the sacrament administered monthly on the first Sunday. All of the services were in Welsh. In 1809 there was a Sunday morning service, with a sermon, and services on all Holy Days and on Wednesdays and Fridays in Lent. From about 1748 the rector also acted as chaplain at Rug, about 1 mile (1.6km) away in the parish of Corwen, where there was an afternoon service on Sundays in 1809. Monthly communicant figures at Llangar averaged about twenty throughout the period, but at Easter this figure rose to between 150 and 200, many of them from neighbouring parishes, especially Gwyddelwern, for many of their parishioners lived nearer to Llangar than to their own parish church. These were very high communicant figures for the period, noticeably

higher than those in surrounding parishes. At one of these, Llanfawr, the vicar noted in 1809 that 'I am sorry to observe that the Number of Communicants is in general but few, except upon the great Festivals when I have had the pleasing satisfaction of communicating with between five and six score at a time'. Even so, this was still fewer than one twentieth of the population of a parish with some 2,400 inhabitants. The population of the parish of Llangar varied only between 32 and 34 families throughout the period, with a firm population figure of 186 given for 1809. The parish had no village, only scattered houses, farms and cottages, and no school. No dissenters were noted until 1809, when a solitary Unitarian and an equally solitary Methodist appear in the returns. This was again unusual for a Welsh parish at this time when the Calvinistic Methodist revival had had a significant impact throughout much of the principality.

The church of All Saints, Llangar, drawn by J. Ingleby in 1794. The drawing shows the dormer window at the western end of the south wall — since removed — which was probably inserted in the early eighteenth century when the west gallery was added; see p. 27 (The National Library of Wales).

Top: The tombstone of Edward Samuel (1674–1748), rector at Llangar between 1721 and 1748, lies next to that of his son, who succeeded him as rector. Samuel was the author of various Welsh poetical and theological works, including Bucheddau'r Apostolion a'r Efengylwyr, *shown above (The National Library of Wales).*

Rectors of Llangar

From the mid-sixteenth century, Llangar's rectors were all Welshmen and seem for the most part to have been resident in their cure. In 1745 the most distinguished of them, Edward Samuel, senior, wrote to the bishop: 'I thank God I have hitherto lived without a curate, but when I want one yr Lordship shall be acquainted with it'. Edward Samuel (1674–1748), author of poetical and theological works in Welsh — of which the most notable was his *Bucheddau'r Apostolion a'r Efengylwyr*, published at Shrewsbury in 1704 — was rector of Betws Gwerful Goch from 1702 until 1721, and thereafter of nearby Llangar until his death. He was succeeded at the latter by his son and namesake.

The elder Samuel was not universally loved by his clerical contemporaries. The Reverend John Wynne, writing in 1730, thought he had 'some brains, but much more conceit… He may be said… to divide his time pretty equally between the glass and the book, between the study and the ale house'. But subsequent Welsh scholars have thought better of him.

The Abandonment of the Church

By the middle of the nineteenth century there was widespread dissatisfaction about the relation of the existing parish churches in the Corwen district of Merionethshire to the actual centres of population. The boundaries of the neighbouring parishes of Gwyddelwern and Llangar were a case in point. Llangar then had a scattered population of 251. Gwyddelwern had a total population of 1,118, about 650 of whom lived at Cynwyd, a village some five miles (8km) from Gwyddelwern church but considerably nearer Llangar. Llangar rectory was then valued at £180 and Gwyddelwern vicarage at £158 10s. per annum. The two parishes had by 1853 agreed to a scheme whereby Cynwyd should be detached from Gwyddelwern and added to Llangar, and it was subsequently determined to build a new church at Cynwyd rather than spend the large sum needed to undertake the restoration of the inconveniently situated parish church at Llangar.

On 11 March 1854 Sir Robert Vaughan of Rug wrote to the bishop of St Asaph: 'I have fixed upon an eligible situation in Cynwyd for the site of the proposed new church there and with your sanction I see no reason why the conveyance of the land should not be proceeded with. I hope shortly to receive a sketch of a suitable church from Mr Rhode Hawkins, architect, London, which I hope may be approved of'. The site was in fact given by Mr Vaughan and on 3 April a public appeal was made for funds to build the church. It was stated that the existing parish church of Llangar was 'in a most dilapidated condition and very inconveniently situated with regard to its present population; and also wholly inadequate to contain the joint population of the two districts', Llangar and Cynwyd. Mr Vaughan himself gave £500, the bishop of St Asaph £100, and various other donors £120; the balance of £147 was made up by the Incorporated Church Building Society. The new church at Cynwyd, dedicated to St John the Evangelist, was consecrated on 5 August 1856 and licensed for marriages in 1864. By 1874 the old church of All Saints was only used for burials, but it was not demolished. The decision to build a new church nearer to the main centre of population had preserved for posterity a perfect pre-Victorian church interior, deprived only of a few of its monuments, which were transferred to its ecclesiastical successor. Llangar church was visited, shortly after its virtual abandonment, by Sir Stephen Glynne, the noted antiquarian and ecclesiologist, on 22 June 1865, and the following entry is recorded in one of his surviving notebooks at St Deiniol's Library, Hawarden. 'This church is now disused and neglected, superceded [sic] by a new one at Cynwyd. It is a long low single building, having the original pointed bell cot with an open arch over the W end and a S porch. The E window Perp[endicula]r, of 3 lights with transom, most of the other windows debased, square headed and small. The doorways are plain with obtuse heads. The font is a plain old circular bowl. There is no west window. The situation is retired and beautiful on sloping ground near to the river Dee'.

No changes would appear to have been made to the building from the date of Sir Stephen's visit until after its transfer into the guardianship of the Welsh Office in 1967, by which time it was in a very poor structural condition. Work on its restoration began in 1974.

Left: The new parish church of Cynwyd, which replaced Llangar following the 1853 rearrangement of parish boundaries to take account of the prevailing centres of population.

Below: The interior of Llangar church before the commencement of the extensive programme of conservation. The coved plaster ceiling was an eighteenth-century addition and has not been replaced (p. 27).

Architectural Development of Llangar Church

Llangar church was taken into State care largely because of the quality of its surviving wall paintings. In 1974 it became clear that the north wall, which — as can be seen today — was leaning precariously, had to be shored up and its footings reinforced. Consequently, it was decided to excavate as much of the interior of the church as possible, and also to undertake a full survey of the surviving architectural features. Conservation of the wall paintings was completed in 1991; in terms of their subject matter and quantity they are unique in north Wales. Based on all the evidence so far assembled, it is now possible to provide a summary of the structural history of the church.

The Medieval Period

The archaeological excavations failed to reveal traces of an earlier church on the site, though a building could have existed nearby. Medieval wall paintings survive on most of the church walls from the western side of the ground-floor north window, along the north, east and south walls, around to a point just east of the south window beneath the gallery (see ground plan, inside back cover).

The earliest of these paintings probably dates to the fourteenth century. At one point along the north wall, the next layer — of fifteenth-century date — extends onto the wallplate. This demonstrates that the four easternmost trusses (the three eastern bays) of the present roof are also medieval. Only the window opening at the east end of the south wall appears to be in approximately its original medieval position.

A cutaway reconstruction drawing showing Llangar church as it may have appeared in the late medieval period. The scheme of paintings within panels along the south wall probably dates from the fifteenth century (Illustration by Jane Durrant).

The Early Seventeenth Century

At various points, mainly at the western end of the church, ancient graffiti can be found cut into the flat faces of the individual stones on the exterior of the church. Some of the carvings are upside down, and in some cases they include dates: six of 1617, three of 1656, and one each of 1615, 1620 and 1654. The frequency of dates between 1615 and 1620 suggests that there may have been a period of repair and rebuilding at Llangar in the early years of the seventeenth century.

The porch was probably also added at this time, as a graffito dated to 1617 can be seen in the western jamb of its doorway, and there are two other dates within the porch of 1617 and 1620. A date of 1617 can also be found on the exterior face at the eastern end of the south wall. The main window in the south wall and an earlier two-light version of the north window may date to this period. So, too, might the large east window, although this could be a little later.

Mid- to Late Seventeenth Century

Sometime during the second half of the seventeenth century, the western end of the church (see ground plan, inside back cover) had to be rebuilt. This was perhaps necessary as a result of structural weakness in the main wall, which is here built on made-up ground. The two subsequently blocked windows to the west of the north door, along with the doorway itself, were probably all inserted at this time.

Early Eighteenth Century

It seems the parish found it necessary to rebuild the western wall for a second time, probably in the early years of the eighteenth century. It was at this time that the two windows above and to the west of the north doorway were blocked up. The opportunity was also taken to insert the west gallery with its dormer window and stone staircase.

A date of 1702 on its single truss suggests that the porch was also reroofed at this time. The survey of 1730 (p. 22) mentions that the north window had lately been enlarged. The style of this window is very similar to that at the western end of the south wall, and suggests that both were inserted during this phase of work.

The Eighteenth and Early Nineteenth Centuries

The final phase of alterations to the church involved the construction of a coved plaster ceiling, which obscured the canopy of honour (p. 32) at the eastern end of the church, and extended west to the front of the gallery. This ceiling, together with the nineteenth-century partitioning, which divided up both the gallery and the area beneath it, were removed during conservation work and have not been replaced.

Left: A detail of one of the graffiti in the porch at Llangar. Dates of 1617 and 1620 indicate that the porch was probably added in the early years of the seventeenth century.

The exterior of Llangar church from the north-west, showing the building fully conserved and lime washed. The sharp drop in the level of the land at the west end appears to have been the cause of subsidence, and necessitated several phases of reconstruction during the seventeenth and eighteenth centuries.

A Tour of Llangar Church

The Churchyard

The pathway leading to Llangar church, which is terraced into the hillslope, takes visitors through the sturdy eighteenth-century stone lich-gate. Such roofed gateways were used by mourners to rest a coffin when arriving at the churchyard (Anglo-Saxon *lych* means corpse). Within, the graveyard at Llangar is of considerable interest since it has been left virtually untouched since the abandonment of the old church for burial after about 1870.

The majority of the pre-1750 burials lie immediately adjacent to the building on the south side. A substantial number of graves near the north side of the church date from between 1750 and 1800. After that date, it seems the burial area was extended to cover the whole of the churchyard except for the north-west corner.

A detailed analysis of the gravestones has revealed that, although before about 1825 the majority of inscriptions are in English, thereafter the bulk were carved in Welsh. This represents an interesting social comment on the parishioners; although its significance is not entirely clear, it may reflect the widespread use of Welsh as a written language for the first time. In addition to the graves, which cover the whole of the period from about 1600 to about 1900, the churchyard also contains the remains of a sundial base.

The Exterior of the Church

The best way for visitors to understand the architectural history of Llangar church is to begin at the porch on the south side of the building and then to proceed around the exterior in an anti-clockwise direction.

The first thing to notice about the building is the sloping nature of the site. This means that the church

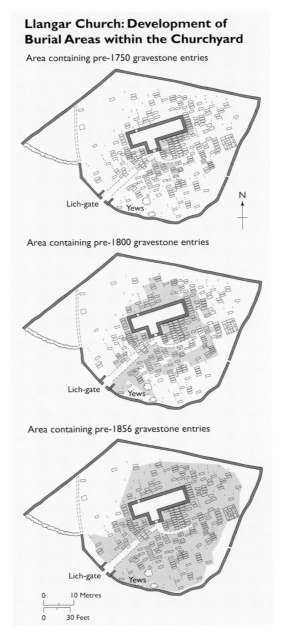

Llangar Church: Development of Burial Areas within the Churchyard

Area containing pre-1750 gravestone entries

Lich-gate   Yews   N

Area containing pre-1800 gravestone entries

Lich-gate   Yews

Area containing pre-1856 gravestone entries

Lich-gate   Yews

0   10 Metres

0   30 Feet

Opposite: Llangar church is approached from the south-west via a pathway terraced into the hillslope, and entered through the lich-gate. Most of the gravestones visible to the south of the church date from before 1750.

The eighteenth-century roofed stone lich-gate at Llangar. Here, at the churchyard entrance, mourners could pause in shelter and rest a coffin before entering the church.

Llangar church is effectively terraced into the hillside, which slopes away towards the river Dee in the valley bottom beyond. This somewhat precarious location accounts for the subsidence that has affected the church and led to the rebuilding of the west end on two separate occasions.

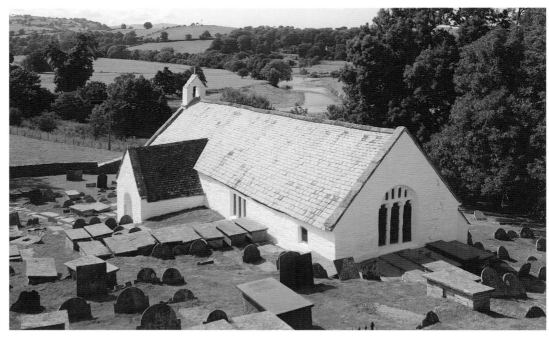

Below: The initials E:M carved with the date 1617, close to the south-east corner of Llangar Church.

Bottom: This small fragment of painted glass in the form of a flower survives in the upper part of the east window at Llangar. Although the window form indicates that it is probably of early seventeenth-century date, the glass is likely to belong to the late seventeenth or early eighteenth century.

is, in effect, built into the hillside, with much of the eastern section of the building well below the level of the churchyard. Originally, material was dug out from the east end of the church platform and dumped at the west. Although this created a level surface on which to build the church, the soft, less consolidated ground at the west end was probably the cause of subsequent structural problems. Similarly, the sloping site may have been responsible for the north wall eventually leaning out from the vertical.

Moving eastwards from the porch, we know from the evidence of the paintings on its inner face that the south wall dates from the medieval period. The main three-light window on this wall probably dates to the early seventeenth century. The small window further to the east (right) appears to be in the position of an earlier opening, the medieval date of which is shown by the painted border around its splays, inside the church. Moving on, just before the corner of the building you will find a stone bearing the initials E:M with the date 1617.

Around the corner (where the grave of Edward Samuel is to be seen, p. 24), the large east window of the church probably dates to the early seventeenth century. It is of a debased Perpendicular type, found elsewhere in Wales, and demonstrates the survival of the Gothic style well into the post-Reformation

period. The window contains a small fragment of painted glass, in the form of a flower, in one of the upper lights. This fragment probably belongs to the late seventeenth or early eighteenth century.

The north-eastern corner of the church has been rebuilt, but we cannot be sure of the date of this work. From the plan (inside back cover), you will see that the whole eastern half of the north wall is now masked by the modern buttress, which is faced in stone and supports the leaning masonry. The only feature of any importance to be lost to view by this essential remedial work is a blocked narrow window. This lies behind the painted cupboard at this point in the interior of the church (p. 34).

Moving west, the window at the end of the buttress was probably inserted sometime during the early eighteenth century. It may have replaced an earlier two-light window, the head and sill of which are just visible above and below the left side of the present window. Below the right-hand corner of this same window, you will see a clear difference between the smaller, more irregular masonry of the medieval wall, and the larger stones used at the west end of the church during its first rebuilding in the second half of the seventeenth century.

Further to the west, traces of the two windows which were blocked up in the early eighteenth century can be seen above and about 5 feet (1.5m) to the right of the north doorway. In the case of the westernmost window, the straight vertical line of the eastern jamb lies along the line of a distinctive break. This break stretches from the top to the bottom of the wall, and marks the extent to which the second rebuilding of the west end of the church extended eastwards. In the area above and between the door and the window jamb can be seen one of the examples of the upside-down graffiti: 'Thomas Lloyd 1656'.

Before leaving the north doorway, it is worth noting that its head is made from a single stone and the jambs consist of exceptionally large roughly dressed blocks. Although the doorway is within the area of the first rebuild, and the door — with its contemporary iron straps and studding — is probably of late seventeenth-century date, the style of the stonework may indicate that it is a reconstruction of an earlier doorway.

As it stands, the west gable wall of the church appears to be part of the second rebuild at this end. Two inserted stones bear the dates 1617 and 1654. The window lighting the gallery has subsequently been reduced from three openings to one. There are entries in the churchwarden's accounts for 1739–42

relating to the casting and hanging of the church bell in the bellcote which surmounts the gable.

Turning the corner, it seems probable that all the masonry to the west (left) of the two-light window in the southern wall, along with the window itself, form part of the second rebuild. A section of the outer face of the wall, extending from the window to the porch, belongs to the first rebuild. The extant medieval wall paintings on the inner face of this stretch, along with graffiti dating to 1615, 1617, and 1656, point to a refacing rather than a more extensive reconstruction of the walls at this point.

The porch is a fairly handsome structure, large and spacious, with an inner door that dates from the late seventeenth or early eighteenth century. The precise date of the porch itself, however, is uncertain, although it is clearly an addition. Graffiti on the inside of the east wall and on the left (west) jamb of the doorway, with dates of 1617 and 1620, appear to have been cut in situ. This would suggest the porch had been built by this time. It may, therefore, have been constructed as part of the second phase of work at the church. The date on the single roof truss is a clear indication that the porch was reroofed in 1702, and there are further references to work on the porch in the churchwardens' accounts for 1715–16.

The south door within the porch at Llangar. The porch was probably added in the early seventeenth century and contains several examples of graffiti and an englyn (verse), dated 1654, written by local poet, Mathew Owen.

The west end of the north wall at Llangar. Traces of two blocked windows can be seen above (1), and to the right (2), of the north door (3). A distinctive break (4), extending from the top to the bottom of the wall, marks the eastwards extent of the second rebuilding of the west end of the church.

Llangar Church: Ground Plan

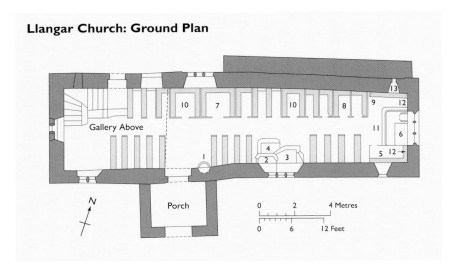

Opposite: The view eastwards from the gallery in Llangar church. This was a parish church, first built in the medieval period. The later fittings are simple, and reveal an emphasis on the pulpit and preaching, rather than the altar.

Below: Part of the canopy of honour at Gyffin church, near Conwy, which is painted with figures of the twelve apostles and the four evangelical symbols. Canopies of honour of this type were fairly common in north Wales and that at Llangar is in part original (ffotograff Photo Library).

The Interior of the Church

The interior of Llangar church is of somewhat greater interest than the exterior. It contains an important series of wall paintings dating from as early as the fourteenth century, through to the second half of the eighteenth century (pp. 35–37), a roof with its origins in the late medieval period, and an almost complete group of eighteenth-century fittings.

Before 1974, the fine open timber roof was hidden by a much-decayed eighteenth-century plaster ceiling. It is difficult to give a precise date for the earliest part of the surviving roof, but a small area of the fifteenth-century wall-painting extends onto the wallplate at the east end of the north wall, indicating that it must have been in existence by that time. The roof runs the whole length of the church, though it has been much altered. The four easternmost trusses are original, but the remainder have been renewed since 1974. Clearly, much of the western half of the roof had been altered in the second half of the seventeenth and early eighteenth centuries, and the need to replace damaged timber since 1974 has resulted in the present mixture of old and new wood in the rafters of the roof.

Over the easternmost bay, the roof has been ceiled with a canopy of honour over the altar, of which only the northern quarter is entirely original. Canopies of honour of this type are fairly common in north Wales. The finest example, thought to date

from the late fifteenth or early sixteenth century, can be seen in St Benedict's church at Gyffin, near Conwy. It is painted with figures of the twelve apostles and the symbols of the four evangelists.

The whole of the floor of the church at Llangar is flagged with rough slabs. There is a substantial slope along the length of the building, the east end being approximately 1 foot 8 inches (0.5m) higher than the west end.

The majority of the internal fittings date from the first half of the eighteenth century. The only earlier piece of furniture is the remarkably crude, probably late medieval, font set into the wall of the church near the south door (**1**). This arrangement clearly post-dates 1732, since at that date the font was freestanding, with a cover, situated near the pulpit. The pulpit as it stands now, in roughly the middle of the south wall, and with the typical eighteenth-century arrangement of pulpit (**2**), reading desk (**3**) and clerk's seat (**4**), also post-dates 1732. At that time, the reading desk, which is made up from pieces of seventeenth-century panelling, stood within the altar rails (p. 22). The present clerk's seat is probably a cut-down version of an earlier pulpit, described as low and incommodious in 1730, in which case it was, according to the churchwardens' accounts, made up in 1726. The present pulpit is presumably the new one described as large and handsome in 1732, and the likelihood is that the present three-decker arrangement was effected very shortly after 1732 to make more room at the east end so as to permit the communicants to receive the sacrament at the altar rails, rather than having it administered to them in their seats. It would seem reasonable to suppose that the font, for which there would now have been no room near the pulpit, was set into the wall near the south door at the same time.

The seating arrangements in Llangar church are particularly interesting. With the exception of the pew (**5**) on the south side of the altar (**6**) — which was the one appropriated to the rector's family — all the pews are situated on the north wall of the church. Along the south wall, on both sides of the pulpit, there are only open benches.

Four of the pews are dated: two with the dates carved in the wood (1711 and 1759), one painted (1841), and the fourth has the date inset in metal (1768). The earliest of these (**7**) is an elaborate affair, made up from seventeenth-century carved panels,

with a coat of arms and the legend 'Cymmer yn Edeirnion'; it belonged to the Hughes family who lived at Gwerclas. The pew dated 1759 (**8**) is carved 'W.J. Cefn cymer', and that of 1768 (**9**) carries the inscription 'IPP.Esqr'. Painted on the door to the pew (**5**) on the south side of the altar is 'The Rectory 1841'.

Two of the undated pews (**10**) have fluted columns on either side of their doors and are probably later than 1750. The remaining pews are more simple boxes. The benches along the south side of the church were made up in the eighteenth

Right: The eighteenth-century cupboard in the north wall of the church, alongside the altar. Equipped with three locks, it probably housed the church plate and registers.

Below right: The rare example of a four-sided — pyramidal — music stand in the west gallery, which would have been used by the choir or church band.

Below: The font at Llangar is set into the south wall of the church. Although probably of late medieval origin, the present arrangement post-dates 1732 when the font was known to be positioned near the pulpit.

century but clearly reuse a certain amount of old wood. It is likely that all the box pews represent the seats in the church belonging to particular houses in the parish. The open benches would have been for the poor, servants, strangers and children.

The east end of the church is, even with the removal of the reading pew after 1732, still extremely cluttered. The altar (**6**) is a simple wooden table made up in the eighteenth century from seventeenth-century pieces, and with plain panelling forming a reredos at the back. The altar is surrounded by rails on three sides (**11**), also eighteenth century, with columns bunched at the corners and an opening in the middle. On either side of the east window are wooden panels with the Ten Commandments inscribed on them in Welsh (**12**). We cannot be certain these are the same boards that were noted as hanging from the roof in 1730 (p. 22), or whether they are replacements, though the letter form is similar to that of inscriptions painted on the walls in the 1730s.

To the north of the altar is an eighteenth-century painted cupboard (**13**). It is decorated with a cherub above, and is equipped with three locks. It was probably used for keeping safe the church plate and registers at a time when there was no vestry provided, and in preference to a church chest.

At the back of the church stone steps lead up to the gallery, which seems to have been fitted out with benches in its present form in 1715–16. The front of the gallery was painted with texts but these are now very faint. It is likely, however, that they are biblical references to the role of music in the worship of God, since the gallery — with its crude eighteenth-century benches — was clearly intended to be used by the singers and those who accompanied them. Indeed, amongst the fittings in the gallery there is a rare and particularly interesting example of a four-sided (pyramidal) music stand, used by the choir or church band.

Before 1974, the area under the gallery was partitioned off to form a vestry. However, this partitioning, which dated from the early nineteenth century, had rotted very badly and was not replaced. In this respect the church has been returned to its eighteenth-century internal arrangement.

The seating in this area, below the gallery, consists of open benches. The seat of one of these, on the north side, has a crude unfinished inscription: T.S:E.R:168.

The Wall Paintings

A. J. Parkinson MA, FSA

Before the Reformation, church services were in Latin and the congregations were generally illiterate; wall paintings and other forms of imagery, such as stained glass, were used as part of the teaching ministry of the church. They would include scenes from the Bible (particularly the life of Christ), incidents from the lives of saints, and moralistic pictures instructing the faithful how to live. Common subjects were the Last Judgement and St Christopher. It was believed that anyone who looked on the picture of St Christopher was safe from danger for that day, so his picture was often placed opposite the main door of the church.

After the Reformation these paintings were destroyed or painted over, since it was thought that there was a real danger of people worshipping the painted images rather than the true God. An Order in Council (1547) required 'the obliteration and destruction of all popish and superstitious books and images…', and later Orders laid down that the Ten Commandments and 'chosen sentences' from the Bible and the Prayer Book should be displayed on the walls of every church. The Royal Arms were also put up, though most examples date from after the Restoration of 1660.

The paintings as we now see them at Llangar bear little relationship to how they were originally meant to be viewed. They were designed to be teaching aids, not 'works of art', and would have been touched up if they became faded, or completely repainted if necessary. Hence, one may discover many layers of painting of different dates, which were never meant to be visible at the same time.

The Dates of the Paintings

There seem to have been at least eight schemes of decoration at Llangar. Two or more are of pre-Reformation date. The earliest, possibly fourteenth

At least eight schemes of wall painting have been identified at Llangar. This section of the north wall shows at least three phases: to the left is a bishop (G), perhaps dating from the fourteenth century, overlain by fifteenth-century decorated framing that encloses scenes possibly from the life of Christ (H), which, in turn, is overlain by an eighteenth-century decorative border containing the Lord's Prayer (L).

Llangar Church: Wall Paintings

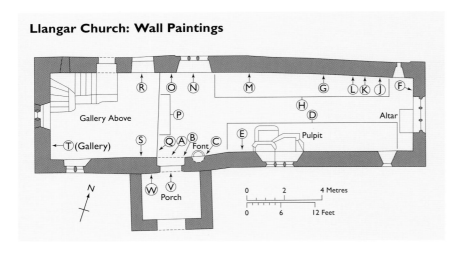

Top right: A bishop, perhaps painted in the fourteenth century, shown in the doorway of an elaborate church (G).

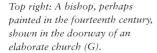

A detail of one of the fifteenth-century painted panels on the south side of the church (D), depicting the Seven Deadly Sins: a boar (Gluttony).

century, are the bishop (**G**) and the figure (**B**) by the south doorway. The possible St Christopher (**S**) and the scenes on the north (**H**) and the south (**D**) walls may be fifteenth century and perhaps not contemporary. The next phases run from the late sixteenth century to the end of the seventeenth century, by which time parts of the walls were concealed by pews. Two phases of texts appear in the angular Gothic style known as 'black-letter' (**C, F, T**), used in printed books until at least 1600. Then follows an *englyn* (a form of stanza in four lines, composed according to strict rules of metre, rhyme and accent) of 1654 in the porch (**W**), and two texts (**C, T**), probably of late seventeenth-century date. Finally, there are two or three phases after 1730, one within the 1730s (**A, N**), which may include the Royal Arms (**M**); another dated 1764, which includes several texts (**Q, P**); in between, possibly dating from 1748 (the year of Edward Samuel's death, p. 24), is the figure of Death (**O**).

A Brief Description

Paintings have been discovered on almost every wall of the church. Above the south doorway is one of four dated inscriptions (**A**) recording the name of the churchwarden. Just to the east is the outline of a man's head (**B**), possibly of fourteenth-century date; the rest of the picture is concealed by a series of texts, (**C**), none sufficiently complete for decipherment, but apparently in Welsh like all others at Llangar. The earliest is pre-1600, a black-letter text in a cable-pattern border; over that is painted another text in a border of strong black and yellow

scrolls, and finally there are traces of a text in brown lettering in an oval frame.

Most of the remainder of the south wall is covered by a series of panels (**D**) outlined in red and probably of fifteenth-century date. Figures survive in some of the upper panels, apparently representing personifications of the Seven Deadly Sins riding symbolically appropriate animals. Of the original seven, only a lion (Pride), a boar (Gluttony) and a stag or goat (Lechery) can be recognized. The last of these was formerly covered by the border (**E**) of an inscription, probably of about 1600. This type of 'morality' painting, contrasting good and evil, is not uncommon, but this form of depiction in a series of panels is almost unique, the only parallel example being at Hardwick church, Cambridgeshire. The lower register of panels would probably have contained the equivalent Acts of Mercy (as described in the Parable of the Sheep and the Goats, Matthew 25: 31–46); these are depicted on a contemporary painting at Ruabon church, Wrexham.

On the east wall (**F**) is part of a black-letter inscription of about 1600 in a cabled border. The north wall has another complex series of overlapping paintings. The earliest (**G**) depicts a bishop in a doorway of an elaborate church, perhaps the Temple at Jerusalem; the style of the architecture suggests that it is fourteenth century in date. Over this is an extensive design in two registers (**H**). Decorated framing (not unlike local timber framing) encloses a series of scenes, possibly from the life of a saint or more likely from the life of Christ. The figures have faded, but the few still visible have costume of fifteenth-century style. They were covered by eighteenth-century decorations of several dates. Towards the east end (**J**) is a fragment of the Apostles' Creed; the border of an inscription (**K**) which may date from the 1730s; and the Lord's Prayer (**L**) in a frame, imitating contemporary architectural decoration. Much of the wall between this and the window was taken up by a huge Royal Arms (**M**), between two texts in roundels. The Royal Arms (now detached and displayed in the reception building at nearby Rug) is complete with the lion and unicorn, and was enclosed in an architectural frame; it was probably painted about 1730. Above the window (**N**) is another inscription dated to the 1730s, recording the name of the rector. To the left of this, crammed between the window and the gallery, is a huge figure of Death (**O**), a skeleton holding a winged hourglass and an arrow. Between his legs are a pick and shovel, and above the window is a lighted lamp. Short inscriptions by the hourglass and lamp may refer to the brevity and uncertainty of life.

On the front of the gallery are four inscriptions. Three (**P**) are inside frames (the middle one architectural in form), and are probably Biblical texts. The fourth (**Q**) records the name of the painter, George Pritchard, and the date of his work (1764), which presumably includes the texts on the gallery and all the other paintings in similar frames. Another, incomplete, inscription under the gallery, of the same date, gives the name of the rector and churchwardens (**R**). Opposite it is another fragmentary fifteenth-century painting (**S**), possibly depicting St Christopher; a small figure with a staff may be either a hermit or a fisherman. On the west wall of the gallery is a section of a painting (**T**) which has been detached and repositioned; it was originally located just to the west of the eastern window in the south wall. It is part of two superimposed paintings of the Ten Commandments, the earlier one of about 1600, the latter of the late seventeenth century.

In the porch is a series of three superimposed texts (**V**) partly masked by the roof truss of 1702. The latest is eighteenth century, the earliest possibly about 1600. To the left of the doorway (**W**) is a unique *englyn*. It is dated 1654, and was probably written by the local poet Mathew Owen.

Part of two superimposed paintings of the Ten Commandments, now positioned on the west wall of the gallery (T).

The Royal Arms (M), which were probably painted in about 1730, on the north wall of the church. Today they are housed in the reception building at Rug following their removal and conservation.

A History of Gwydir Uchaf Chapel

The Wynn Family and the Building of the Chapel

The private chapel of Holy Trinity at Gwydir Uchaf, in the parish of Llanrwst, was begun in 1673 by Sir Richard Wynn (d. 1674). The Wynns were one of the most distinguished families in north Wales. The founder of this important dynasty, Maredudd ab Ieuan, had, at the end of the fifteenth century, restored and lived in the castle of Dolwyddelan, some 10 miles (16km) further up the Conwy valley.

His great-grandson, Sir John Wynn (1553–1626), wrote his history of the family in the early seventeenth century. His son, Sir Richard Wynn, was responsible for adding the Gwydir chapel to Llanrwst parish church in 1633–34. It was Sir Richard's nephew and namesake who built the chapel at Gwydir Uchaf.

The Wynns built two houses at Llanrwst. The earlier residence was Gwydir, which for more than 200 years served as the principal seat of the family. Today, it comprises a rather straggling group of buildings varying in date from the early sixteenth to the late nineteenth centuries. In 1604, Sir John Wynn built a new and somewhat smaller house, Gwydir Uchaf. It became more popular with the family, and it was to this second residence that Sir Richard Wynn added his free-standing chapel (see illustration, p. 41). The much altered seventeenth-century house continues to stand nearby (now the Forestry Commission offices).

Sir Richard died without a male heir in 1674, the year after work began on the chapel, and his baronetcy passed to John Wynn of Watstay, now Wynnstay. Sir Richard was survived by his only daughter, Mary, who in 1678 married Robert Bertie, fourth earl of Lindsey, created duke of Ancaster in 1715.

Sir Richard Wynn took a keen personal interest in the building and furnishing of his chapel. In 1673 John Lloyd, afterwards bishop of St Davids, wrote to him, saying: 'I pray let me know how forwards you are with the chapel, which I long to see finished, and hope ere I dye to have your order for an organ for it'. Sir Richard's 'high church' tendencies are revealed in an interesting letter from Father Edward Petre, the Jesuit confessor of the future King James II (1685–88), who wrote in 1674:

I hartly wish I were as able to correspond with your desire in procuring a Cross for your chapel window. I will assure you noe endeavours of mine are, or shall be wanting (if possible) to effect it, thoughe I heare from severall (whom I have imployed att London uppon that account) that ye art is now wholeye lost, and non durable to be gott unlesse out of some old church windowe. I have also written to an intimate friend att Paris, but I doubt to as little purpose, in regard they are less frequent beyond seas, and nothing soe much used there, as here in England.

In 1676 his mother, Lady Grace Wynn, who survived her son by five years, compiled a list of the plate at Caermelwr which included 'a great bowl with a cover double gilt, which I bestowe upon the chappell of Gwydder'. There is no record of the chapel's consecration or licensing, but the above references indicate that, like the almost contemporary chapel of Compton Wynyates in Warwickshire, the chapel at Gwydir Uchaf took some years to be completed and fully furnished.

The chapel was noted by a number of antiquarians and travellers between the late seventeenth and early nineteenth centuries. Edward Lhuyd in his *Parochialia* (of about 1690) noted that 'there's a chappell belonging to the House of Gwydir just by the house endow'd with a sallary of £4 a year. This is generally given to the head school-master'.

Dr Pococke in 1757 was complimentary: 'near the house is a very handsome chapel'. Bingley in 1800

Opposite: The seventeenth-century chapel of Holy Trinity at Gwydir Uchaf, begun by Sir Richard Wynn in 1673.

Maredudd ab Ieuan — the fifteenth-century founder of the Wynn dynasty. This illustration depicts Maredudd as he appears on his memorial brass in the church at Dolwyddelan, close to the castle which he had restored and inhabited.

The interior of Gwydir Uchaf chapel looking towards the western gallery, which is supported on a massive beam decorated with alternate roundels and rectangles, similar to those adorning the gallery at Rug. The late seventeenth-century domestic chairs provided seating in the wide central aisle between the two pew blocks.

was wholly dismissive, however: 'the family chapel is still left; this is a small building in the Gothic style, sufficiently neat on the outside, but the roof and some other parts are decorated with paintings of scriptural figures, most miserably executed'. The chapel was visited by Sir Stephen Glynne on 5 September 1867, and he recorded the following remarks in his notebook:

This is curious as a Post-Reformation ecclesiastical building. It has the date 1673 over the north door, and much resembles the contemporary chapel in Llanrwst Church. It is an oblong room, undivided. The lateral windows are three lights with plain mullions. The east

window is of four lights with rather flat Pointed arch. The roof is coved and boarded, painted with figures of angels, etc. The lower part of each wall is wainscoted, the altar has a fair wood-carving, as also the prayer-desk, and at the west end is a gallery with open balustrade. The north doorway has a round arch.

Gwydir estate records indicate that up to 1920, when regular services ceased to be held in the chapel, the rector of the adjoining parish of Trefriw had been paid a salary as chaplain. In 1952 Grimsthorpe Estates Limited, representing the third earl of Ancaster, transferred the chapel to the guardianship of the Ministry of Works, and it is now maintained by Cadw.

A Tour of Gwydir Uchaf Chapel

The Exterior of the Chapel

Gwydir Uchaf chapel stands on a relatively flat shelf of land amid thick surrounding woodland which rises steeply from the Conwy valley. The ground plan of the chapel (inside back cover) is essentially a plain rectangle, with no formal division between the nave and chancel. As we shall see, the proportions of the building, together with the west gallery and certain other internal details, are similar to those noted at Rug chapel.

The exposed exterior walls of the chapel are built chiefly of a yellowish sandstone ashlar. Some local slate is also used, especially in the west wall and below the plain chamfered plinth on the other sides. The masonry has a quality and character unusual in the district. The roof, of thick slates with a stone ridge, is original. The bellcote at the west end is probably original also, but the bell is dated 1752.

The doorway in the north wall has a round head with a continuous moulding, and there is a lozenge decoration at the base of the jambs. Above the doorway, a stone panel bears a shield inscribed SRWB 1673, the letters standing for Sir Richard Wynn, baronet. The studded door with decorated strap hinges is original. The frames and mullions of the chapel windows are of wood, and were originally covered in a thin coat of plaster to imitate stone. You will also see a decorative heart carved at the base of the surrounding stone chamfer on each side of the main windows. At the west end of the chapel, below the bellcote, there is a much plainer square-headed window.

A few yards to the west of the chapel, on the rising ground, are the somewhat denuded remains of a low 'ziggurat'. This once ornamental mound is probably a relic of the seventeenth-century gardens attached to Gwydir Uchaf house.

The Interior of the Chapel

As at Rug, the plain and almost Gothic appearance of the exterior in no way prepares the visitor for the decorative details within. The whole is dominated by

Left: The house and chapel of Gwydir Uchaf as depicted by Thomas Dineley in the late seventeenth-century. There appears to have been some licence taken in showing the relationship of the chapel to the house (The National Library of Wales).

Below: One of the decorative carved hearts found on the base of the stone chamfer on each of the main windows at Gwydir Uchaf. This is the best-preserved example and can be found on the south-east window of the chapel.

Left: The studded door in the north wall dates from the foundation of the chapel in 1673 by Sir Richard Wynn. This is commemorated by the carved stone panel above the doorway, which carries the date and founder's initials.

Gwydir Uchaf Chapel: Ground Plan

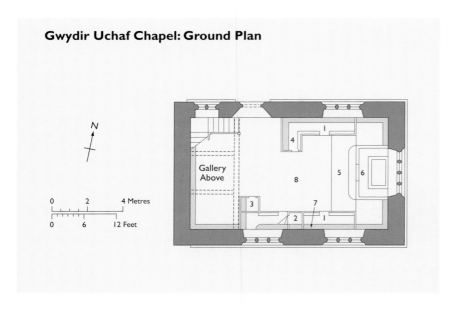

Above right: The carved wooden cartouche above the gallery on the west wall of Gwydir Uchaf chapel.

One of the more robust, locally produced oak figures on the pulpit.

the quite striking baroque painted ceiling, which is described below. The walls are plastered above a panelled dado, and the original floor was at a slightly lower level than the present flagstones.

At the west end is the gallery, where a small band with singers probably provided the music for the services. The gallery is supported on a massive beam embellished with carved and painted strap decoration in the form of alternate roundels and rectangles. In the centre of this decoration is a shield, inscribed as that above the external door, but with a lozenge above and a heart below. The gallery parapet is formed of a heavy moulded rail supported on sturdy turned balusters, with solid, lozenge-decorated panels in the centre and at each end. Access to the gallery is by a stair of two straight flights against the north and west walls. The design of this stair, particularly the early form of the narrow handrail and its clumsy fitting in the gallery, suggest that it may have been used previously elsewhere.

Near the top of the west wall, above the gallery, there is a carved wooden cartouche or panel. Below a cherub's head, there is an incomplete Latin inscription from John 10: 27:

OVES MEAE	My sheep
VOCEM MEAM	hear my
AUDIUNT	voice
[ET EGO COGNOSCO EAS]	[and I know them]
ET SEQVUNTUR ME	and they follow me

Beneath the gallery is a low, panelled dado of poplar, with a bench attached. The dado is returned under the stairs to form a cupboard. Although of early form, with small plain panels and solid moulded frames, it was fixed in its present position after the wall had been plastered, and the floor raised. East of the gallery the walls are panelled, or wainscoted, in spruce to a height of 7 feet 9 inches (2.7m).

The plain panels have a small applied moulding and are of later character than the work under the gallery, but the bold projecting cornice, which is carried through into the window reveals, is very similar to that skirting the base of the ceiling. There are finely-carved lime wood cherubs (of varying style and design) fixed to a number of corners on the panelling.

The liturgical arrangements of the interior are of some interest, since the pews (**1**) are planned on collegiate lines facing a central aisle. This arrangement was a very common one in private chapels of the late seventeenth, eighteenth and early nineteenth centuries. A few parish churches were also built or refitted with these arrangements. There are examples virtually contemporary with Gwydir Uchaf at Knole in Kent, Belton House in Lincolnshire, Petworth House in Sussex, Woodhey in Cheshire and Halton in Shropshire. At Gwydir Uchaf the pulpit (**2**) is placed in the middle of the southern pew block, with the reading desk (**3**) in the returned position at the west end of the same block. The return is matched at the west end of the shorter northern pew block (**4**) and

serves to preserve the occupants from any draughts coming through the north door. Seventeenth-century carved oak figures fixed to the sides of the pulpit have a local and more robust character than those attached to the walls.

A section of the paving slabs at the east end of the floor (**5**) has been laid in a diagonal pattern, and the communion rails (**6**) have been raised on a step. The oak rails, which are turned to the east wall, have a central gate; the flat-top rail is carried on heavy turned balusters and square corner posts set on a solid sill.

The communion table from the chapel (see illustration) bears the date 1641, but is largely a modern reconstruction. The bulbous legs may be original but the guilloche and the other enrichment are applied in thin strips.

Fixed to the south wall above the dado is a framed panel bearing the arms of King Charles II (1660–85), with supporters, crest and motto (**7**). This is well painted in colour and forms a strong contrast to the piety of the ceiling.

In the original arrangement the wide central aisle (**8**) between the two pew blocks would probably have been filled with chairs. Wide central aisles with space for chairs or loose benches were a common feature of many eighteenth-century town churches. They provided additional accommodation if required but had the added convenience of being removable if the space was needed for other purposes.

One of the cut-out angels at Gwydir Uchaf, bearing part of the Great Doxology – ET IN TERRA PAX, IN HO :&C (and peace on earth to men of goodwill).

The Painted Ceiling

The ceiling at Gwydir Uchaf belongs to a vigorous tradition of seventeenth-century painted ceilings, of which there are numerous examples in Scandinavia, several in Scotland (Grandtully, for example), and important English examples at Staunton Harold, Leicestershire (1653), Bromfield, Shropshire (1672) and Queenborough, Kent (1695). A lost example, dated 1661, is also known from Llangadwaladr on Anglesey.

Although the paintings at Gwydir Uchaf are crudely executed, there can be little doubt that they are inspired by the Italian baroque rather than traditional vernacular or local folk art. Sir Richard Wynn was in touch with Continental affairs, and it may well be that the design was suggested by one of his high Anglican or Roman Catholic friends, and executed by local craftsmen. The paintings are executed in a glue tempera on wooden boards which have their joints sealed with cotton tapes. The paintings cover the entire ceiling, together with the apex of the east wall, and have been particularly well preserved. The theme is an ambitious one, embracing the whole of divine self-revelation. The boarded top of the east wall symbolizes the creation, showing the heavens and firmament, and night and day. These flank a demi-glory (half of a halo) containing the Hebrew Tetragrammaton (the Hebrew name for God, vocalized as Jehovah or Jahweh).

The three eastern roof bays represent the Persons of the Trinity, indicative of the chapel's dedication; their emblems, surrounded by four cherubs, occupy the flat central panels of each bay. The flanking side panels contain robust angels disporting themselves on cushiony clouds. The bay over the gallery warns the spectator of the Day of Judgement. To the base of each truss is fixed, in medieval style, a flat cut-out angel, reminiscent of those at Rug. Each one holds between outstretched hands a scroll bearing Latin invocations or prayers.

The east bay has in the centre the sacred Christian monogram IHS, a cross and pierced heart, all enclosed within a glory or halo. Below, in the side panels, the angels have one hand raised pointing to Heaven and the other down to Earth. The cut-out angels carry the inscriptions VENERANDVM NOMEN IESVS (The name of Jesus is to be venerated) on the south, and PER HOC NOMEN ET NON PER ALIVD (by this name and by no other) on the north.

The next bay shows in the centre the seated figure of God the Father, with the feet towards the east; in addition to a halo with rays of glory, the upper part of the body is encased in a larger glory. Below, the kneeling angels are worshipping God, their arms raised aloft in prayer. The cut-out angels carry the Great Doxology, GLORIA IN EXCELSIS DEO (Glory to God in the highest) on the south, and ET IN TERRA PAX, IN HO :&C [= *Hominibus bonae voluntatis*] (and peace on earth [to men of goodwill]) on the north.

The third bay from the east depicts the Holy Ghost in the form of the dove, flying westwards and set in a glory. This bay, instead of the usual pattern of stars, has tongues of fire, representing the coming of the Holy Spirit on the day of Pentecost (described in Acts 2: 3, as 'cloven tongues like as of fire'). Below, the angels, dressed in white, are in a relaxed attitude, with their hands outstretched in a gesture of dispensation, and their wings raised. The cut-out angels carry the opening words of the Latin hymn used at Vespers on the Vigil of Pentecost: VENI SPIRITVS SANC[TE] (Come Holy Spirit) on the south and ET REPLE CORDA FIDELIVM (and fill the hearts of the faithful) on the north.

The bay over the gallery contains two trumpeting angels announcing the Day of Judgement. Against the west wall is a demi-glory enclosing the sacred emblem INRI (*Iesus Nazarenus Rex Iudaeorum*) and a cross *formée*. From this radiates a long, tapering banner on which is written WATCH FOR YOU KNOW NOT YE DAY OR HOWRE (Matthew 25: 13).

Opposite: A section from the baroque-inspired painted ceiling at seventeenth-century Gwydir Uchaf chapel. This panel shows the seated figure of God the Father surrounded by four cherubs.

Right: A diagrammatic representation of the painted ceiling at Gwydir Uchaf.

Derwen Churchyard Cross

L. A. S. Butler MA, PhD, FSA

South of the church of Saint Mary at Derwen stands a fine late medieval cross, probably dating from the mid- to late fifteenth century. Its main purpose was to serve as a focal point to encourage devotion to the Crucified Christ, particularly on Palm Sunday (the last Sunday before Easter), and to the Virgin Mary, at Annunciation (25 March), Visitation (2 July), Nativity (8 September), and, especially, the Assumption (15 August).

The cross stands on a square plinth approached by two tiers of steps, rising in height to almost 15 feet (4.3m) so that it dominates the surrounding churchyard. The plinth consists of a single stone, the upper corners of which have been cut at an angle — chamfered — to create broach stops. An octagonal shaft, 7 feet (2m) high, rises from the plinth and this, too, has been cut from a single squared pillar of stone. The corners have been chamfered to create faces of unequal size and are decorated with raised bosses in the form of human heads and foliage.

Bosses depicting similar motifs decorate the capital at the top of the shaft; below the bosses, sinuous tongues of stylized foliage point down the shaft.

The head of the cross is rectangular: the wider east and west faces each consist of a double niche and the narrower north and south faces a single one. The top of the cross is ornamented with traceried pinnacles, but the apex has been damaged. In contrast, the lower part of the head is ornamented with rosettes where it narrows sharply to meet the capital. The carved decoration on the four faces of the cross is remarkably well preserved: that on the west face shows the Crucifixion with the Virgin Mary and Saint John; that on the east face is thought to depict the Coronation of the Virgin. The Virgin Mary and the Christ Child appear on the north face and on the south face there is a figure with weighing scales and an upraised sword — probably the Archangel Michael weighing souls on Judgement Day.

Opposite: Derwen churchyard cross stands to the south of the now redundant church of Saint Mary, Derwen, in the Vale of Clwyd. The cross was most probably erected in the second half of the fifteenth century to encourage devotion to the Crucified Christ and the Virgin Mary. All four faces of the head are highly decorated; that to the east, shown in this view, is thought to depict the Coronation of the Virgin.

Far left: The Crucifixion is shown on the west face of the cross, flanked by the figures of the Virgin Mary and Saint John.

Middle: The figure shown on the south face, carrying weighing scales and an upraised sword, is probably the Archangel Michael, weighing souls on Judgement Day.

Left: The north face of the cross is carved with the figures of the Virgin Mary and Christ Child.

Top: The unusual hexagonal-shaped fourteenth-century cross-head from the church of Saint Saeran, Llanynys, Denbighshire. This face is carved with the Crucified Christ; the figure of a bishop appears on the reverse.

Bottom: The highly decorated head of the churchyard cross at the church of Saint Chad, Hanmer, Wrexham. Like the cross at Derwen, the head is rectangular, and two faces are carved with the Crucifixion (shown here) and the Virgin Mary and Christ Child.

Depictions of the Crucifixion and of the Virgin Mary were sometimes defaced at the Reformation or, more often, in the Civil War (1642–48). Fortunately, the remoteness of Derwen has ensured the survival of the cross, but it did suffer damage when the village school was kept in the lich-gate and schoolboys, two centuries ago, would climb the shaft, using the carved heads as footholds, and sit upon the head of the cross.

Within the church there is a well-preserved late fifteenth-century rood loft and screen, on which the carved wooden figures of the Crucifixion scene would have been prominent.

Historical Background

In the early Middle Ages, pillar crosses were erected over graves or as boundary markers, for example, the ninth-century Pillar of Eliseg, near Valle Crucis Abbey, and the late tenth-century cross of Maen Achwyfan, near Whitford. By the twelfth century, however, crosses were erected in churchyards — such as the twelfth-century cross shaft at Corwen and the fourteenth-century cross-head at Llanynys, between Denbigh and Ruthin. The latter is particularly fine and a predecessor of the late medieval high crosses, such as Derwen. The Llanynys cross-head is a thin slab of stone carved into a hexagonal shape, with the Crucified Christ on one face, and on the other, a bishop — this probably represents St Saeran, the patron saint of the church. Devotion to the Crucified Christ depicted upon a churchyard cross in this way had been recommended as early as 1229 in advice given by William of Blois, bishop of Hereford. Worship to the Virgin Mary as the Mother of God increased during the thirteenth and fourteenth centuries throughout England and Wales, with altars, chapels and crosses being consecrated to her devotion.

These specialized forms of late medieval churchyard cross, with depictions of the Crucifixion and of the Virgin Mary, are known in north-east and south-east Wales, as well as in many other parts of the British Isles. Locally, in the Vale of Clwyd and nearby, there are three other churches worth visiting to inspect their crosses: Hanmer, Llanrhydd and Trelawnyd (Newmarket). Other churchyard crosses survive only as truncated shafts, until recently used to support flat sundial plates.

Further Reading

G. W. O. Addleshaw and F. Etchells, *The Architectural Setting of Anglican Worship* (London 1948).

G. K. Brandwood, 'Anglican Churches before the Restorers', *Archaeological Journal*, **144** (1987), 383–408.

M. Chatfield, *Churches the Victorians Forgot* (Ashbourne 1979).

B. F. L. Clarke, *The Building of the Eighteenth Century Church* (London 1963).

D. Findlay, 'Centralised Plans for Anglican Churches in Georgian England', *Georgian Group Report and Journal* (1989), 66–74.

G. M. Griffiths, editor, *A Report of the Deanery of Penllwyn and Edeirnion by the Reverend John Wynne 1730* (Merioneth Historical and Record Society 1955).

D. B. Hague, 'Rug Chapel, Corwen', *Journal of the Merioneth Historical and Record Society*, **3** (1958), 167–83.

D. B. Hague, *Gwydir Uchaf Chapel* (Welsh Office, Cardiff 1980).

W. M. Jacob, *Lay People and Religion in the Early Eighteenth Century* (Cambridge 1996).

J. Gwynfor Jones, editor, *History of the Gwydir Family*, by Sir John Wynn (Llandyssul 1990).

F. C. Mather, 'Georgian Churchmanship Reconsidered', *Journal of Ecclesiastical History*, **36** (1985), 255–83.

R. Shoesmith, 'Llangar Church', *Archaeologia Cambrensis*, **129** (1980), 64–132.

P. Virgin, *The Church in an Age of Negligence* (Cambridge 1989)

D. Walker, editor, *A History of the Church in Wales* (Historical Society of the Church in Wales 1976).

M. Whiffen, *Stuart and Georgian Churches* (London 1948).

W. N. Yates, 'Church Buildings of the Protestant Establishments in Wales and Scotland: Some Points of Comparison', *Journal of Welsh Ecclesiastical History*, **9** (1992), 1–19.

W. N. Yates, *Buildings, Faith and Worship: The Liturgical Arrangement of Anglican Churches 1600–1900* (Oxford 1991; new edition 2000).

W. N. Yates, 'The Progress of Ecclesiology and Ritualism in Wales', *Archaeologia Cambrensis*, **149** (2000), 59–88.

Derwen Churchyard Cross

Helen Burnham, *A Guide to Ancient and Historic Wales: Clwyd and Powys* (London 1995), 177–88.

Elias Owen, *Old Stone Crosses of the Vale of Clwyd and Neighbouring Parishes* (London and Oswestry 1886), 34–36.

Royal Commission on Ancient Monuments in Wales, *An Inventory of the County of Denbigh* (London 1914), 47–48.